Pierre Dechifre Gilbert Lebrun

Rennes

Editions OUEST-FRANCE

foreword

I decided to live in Rennes, or, at least near it, in 1990. Like a lot of people from western Brittany, I often used to pass through here from being a teenager, but much too quickly to really appreciate how attractive it is. Nevertheless, a rather childish pride always tugged at my heartstrings whenever I found myself in the capital of Brittany.

So, anyway, one of the reasons for my choosing Rennes was the fact that, it seemed quite logical to settle there, travelling to and fro, as I did, between the French capital and western Brittany. Living in the region of the Riedones obviously also had its practical side that is familiar to all the 'new Rennais of the TGV age'.

However, when I had moved here, I was completely won over by Rennes and its region, falling utterly in love with it. Even if I still have one or two regrets about the place, the fact that the river Vilaine is covered over, for example, I love the liveliness of its student life, its modern approach to life with the Metro, the NEC, and the twin tower-blocks of Bourg-L'Evêque, its pedestrian streets, its interior courtyards, the Mordelaise Gate, and the Thabor gardens.

As a citizen of Rennes, I applaud its efforts to establish social cohesiveness and the spirit of community, as well as the obvious importance given to the Breton language. (It is worth noting that the proportion of Breton speakers in Rennes corresponds to the general average within Brittany).

Thank you to Rennes and its region !

Trugarez deoc'h Bro-Roazhon !

Alan Stivell

A

Anne of Brittany

Anne was only 11 years old when she inherited the Duchy of Brittany, an event which led to a great deal of political intrigue. King Charles VIII of France seized Nantes and Guingamp, and his troops besieged Rennes, and so, to save something of the situation, the strong-minded young duchess agreed to marry Charles, the marriage contract of 6 December, 1491 stipulating that from then on Brittany was to remain part of France.
After Charles VIII's death in April, 1498, Anne regained her position as duchess, but this only lasted until her next marriage to Louis XII, Charles VIII's cousin. Anne had eight children during her two marriages, of whom only two, Claude, the future wife of François I, and Renée survived her.

Anne of Brittany's body being carried from Blois to Paris.

Atlantic Arc

Because of the fact that cities such as Glasgow, Cork, Cardiff, Brest, Nantes, Angers, Bordeaux, Bayonne-Anglet-Biarritz, Bilbao, Santiago de Compostella, Braga, Oporto, Lisbon, and Seville share the same geographical position as Rennes, **the cities of the western edge** of the European Union have grouped together to establish a balance in the European development process. They share a common culture, identity, and other resources, and are thereby expressing their desire for stronger corporate action as a network.
The first conference of the cities of the Atlantic Arc took place in Rennes on the 6 and 7 July, 2000.

Rennes Atalante Science & Technology Park was set up by Rennes District in 1984. It comprises research and higher education institutes, high technology companies, innovation grant agencies and technology transfer centres and is spread over three sites:

- Rennes Atalante Beaulieu, specialising in information technology (telecommunications, I.T., imaging and electronics).
- Rennes Atalante Champeaux, dedicated to food processing (Europe's No. 1 centre for milk) and the environment.
- Rennes Atalante Villejean, focusing on health (cancerology, medical imaging, neuroscience, drugs, etc.).

In the future:

- Rennes Atalante Saint-Malo
- Rennes Atalante Kerlann

At the end of October 2002, the 230 companies making up Rennes Atalante (whether based at one of the three sites or members of the association with the same name) employed some 13,000 people and created 150 jobs in that year alone.

The Rennes Atalante Beaulieu science park, a centre for the new communication technologies.

Atalante

B

(Bassin de Rennes) Rennes Basin

Rennes lies in an irregularly-shaped basin formed during the Tertiary period. To the south, it rises suddenly with Pont-Réan's sandstone hills, but elsewhere the rise is only gradual - for 15 km northwards, towards Vignoc and Saint-Germain-sur-Ille, 50 km westwards up to Caulnes, and as least as much eastwards. This traditional cattle rearing and arable farming area owes its abundant water supply to the fact that six rivers converge there: the Vilaine, the Ille, and the Flume from the north, the Meu from the north-west, the Blosne from the east, and the Seiche from the south-east.

Beauregard

Beauregard is **the most recent area in Rennes** to be developed, and its 71 hectares will eventually accommodate more than 2,250 housing units. Awareness of environmental quality has been one of this important urban development project's major concerns, and 17 hectares of green open space have been provided. Beauregard is also a showcase for energy-saving techniques. Using earth, hemp, and wood as construction materials, an experimental block of flats, with the rather pretty name of 'Salvatierra', has been built within the framework of a European programme.

(La Bernique hurlante) The Howling Limpet

The old saying that Rennes has as many bars as days in the year is no exaggeration! However, it is not so much the number that is surprising but all the different names. Here is an alphabetical list of bars that you may come across while strolling around Rennes: L'Ailleurs, L'Antalya Café, L'Artiste Assoiffé, L'Art Ty Chaud, Bla Bar, La Bascule, Le Bateau Ivre, La Bernique Hurlante, Le Cactus, Café Némo, Le Chatham, Le Chat qui Pêche, Chez Ma Tante, La Cité d'Ys, Le

Biotechnology

Biotechnology is "the application of science or engineering in the direct or indirect use of living organisms or parts of organisms, either in their natural state or in modified form". Within this field, Rennes specialises in biological engineering, medical imaging, nutrition, cancer research, research into liver disease, plant production, molecular biology, and product development.

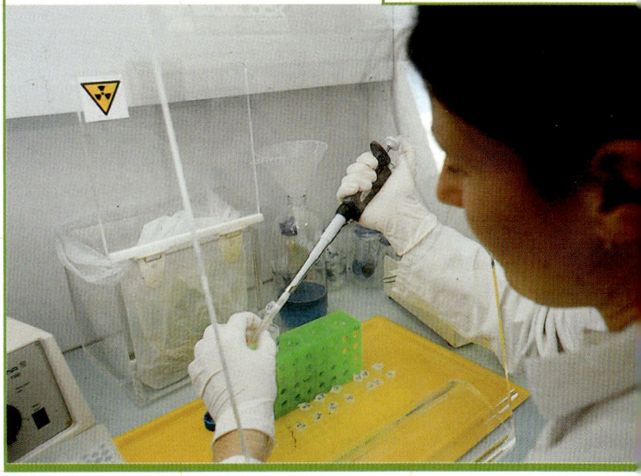

Déjazey, L'Elsa Popping, Le Mâchon Gourmand, Le Mondo Bizzaro, Rennes 1929, Nabuchodonosor, Le Nez Rouge, Le Nozdei, O'Connell's Irish Bar, La Paillote, Le Petit Bazar, Le Petit Caboulot, Le Pyranha, Le Scaramouche, Le Scarron, La Taverne du Haut Grimoire, Le Temps d'un verre, Le Tournebride, Vins et Voyages, Le Zanzibar, Le Zing, Le Zouave...

Blosne (Le)

The La Binquenais area during the 1960s (left) and today (right).

It is often said, and is certainly true, that **Rennes has kept the background of its old rural past.** In any event, throughout the southern part of Rennes are to be found the traces of place-names, as at Le Blosne, where the names that dot the area more or less follow the path of the old farms at Hautes-Ourmes, Landrel, Binquenais, Ecotais, Quineleu, and Poterie.

This rural past is, however, sometimes very recent. This photograph taken in the 1960s shows, for example, the La Binquenais area before it was built up. Today, La Binquenais' college stands on the exact spot where the market gardens of La Petite Thébaudais farm (at the top of the photograph) used to be.

Boulanger (Georges)

Georges Boulanger a very popular, and populist, general and politician was born in Rennes in 1837. He came close to leading a coup d'état against the Third Republic in 1889, but instead backed down and chose to go into exile in Belgium. He committed suicide on his mistress' tomb in Brussels in 1891.

The general, who was born in Rennes, gave his name to the populist political movement of Boulangism.

Buttes de Coësmes

Rising to a height of 73 metres, this is the highest point in Rennes. The 'Télécom' tower, a distinctive landmark when approaching the city from Paris, stands at a height of 180 metres, but lies within the boundaries of Cesson-Sévigné. Within Rennes itself, the tower-blocks of Les Horizons in Bourg-L'Evêque and L'Eperon in the central area of Colombier have rival claims to the title of the city's highest point. Beauregard (63 metres) and Thabor (56 metres) are two other high-standing areas, whilst, at 20 metres, the lowest-lying areas are down at the level of the river Vilaine, near the Lacs d'Apigné.

Capital

"Be that as it may, **I soon learned that Rennes was the capital of Brittany.** And what is a capital ? Isn't it the main city in a country ? Isn't the city of Paris the capital of France ? Some claim, though, that it isn't Rennes that is the capital of Brittany, but Nantes. Nobody believes them. Wasn't Rennes always the seat of the Breton Parliament until the great French Revolution ?" Louis Guilloux. *Ma Bretagne.*

Coat of arms proposed by Rallier du Baty, mayor of Rennes, in 1667.

(Ceinture verte) Green Belt

Where country and city meet. Here, to the south of Rennes, are the agricultural areas of Noyal-Châtillon-sur-Seiche.

Rennes is one of the rare cities in France, if not the only one, not to suffer from suburban sprawl. This is essentially due to the existence of a 'green belt', which separates the city centre, encircled by its ring road, from the outlying towns and villages. This determination to preserve a space to act as a buffer zone around the city boundary has been a constant factor in every single one of Rennes' town plans from the end of the Second World War onwards. This aerial photograph of Le Blosne, bordered by the agricultural area to the south of Rennes, illustrates this perfectly.

Champs libres (Les)

This is the name of the **new cultural complex** built on the site of the former coach station on Esplanade Général-de-Gaulle. The unique complex houses three separate structures the Brittany Museum, city library and Science Centre. The conference hall is an additional feature. To achieve this "three-in-one" complex, the architect Christian de Portzamparc (to whom we also owe the *Cité de la musique* in Paris and the French Embassy in Berlin) combined three geometric shapes – a parallelepiped for the museum, an upside-down pyramid for the library and a dome shape for the Science Centre.

The Brittany Museum, city library and Science Centre have been housed under one roof since 2005.

City centre

R. Volante

H. El Bouhghammi

D. Levasseur

H. El Bouhghammi

olante

B. Volante

D. Levasseur

H. El Boubghammi

Chateaubriand (François René)

"Rennes seemed like a Babylon to me, and the school, a world. The vast numbers of masters and pupils, the size of the buildings, the garden, and the courtyards appeared absolutely enormous... " In his book, *Mémoires d'Outre-tombe* (Memories from beyond the grave), Chateaubriand adopted a tone that was both amused and nostalgic in order to recount his discovery of the 'big city' when he began two years of school at Rennes after spending thirteen years of country childhood at the château of Combourg. Whilst recalling his teachers and his studies, he remembers above all the rumpus of life as a school boarder, his friends, and the scraps and scrapes he was involved in among the trees and bushes "in the garden of the Benedictines, called the *Thabor.*"

He was to take up his pen again to record another incident, that of the meeting of the Estates of Rennes and the January days of 1789 in which he personally took part (see the article on the Revolution).

Cider

In the early 20th century, Ille-et-Vilaine was **the leading cider-making department in France,** producing 400 million litres a year. Cider was by far and away the most popular drink, and played an important part in the daily life of Rennes, a fact which was demonstrated by the many local 'cider cafés' and cellars which can still be seen in the city centre. After a decline in popularity during the 1950s and 1960s, when it was supplanted by (low quality) wine and beer, cider is today winning acclaim thanks to the action of enthusiastic producers for whom quality is paramount. The role played by the Ecomusée du Pays de Rennes (Rennes Museum of Rural Life) in saving local varieties of apples is also worthy of note.

After its decline in popularity from the 1950s onwards, is cider making a comeback in Rennes ?

Citroën

The Janais site was set up in 1961 on 240 hectares of land, 80 of which contained buildings. Today, the company is dedicated to top-of-the-range PSA Group models and employs 10,000 people to manufacture 1,700 vehicles a day.

From the Ami 6 to the C5 – 40 years of Citroën in Rennes.

From 1961 to mid-2004, eleven different models were manufactured on the site, i.e. over 9.2 million vehicles:

- Ami 6 (1961-1971) 1,035,866 vehicles manufactured.
- Ami 8 (1969-1979) 773,344 vehicles.
- GS (1970-1981) 1,874,754 vehicles.
- Visa (1978-1988) 1,222,608 vehicles.
- GSA (1979-1987) 565,009 vehicles.
- BX (1982-1994) 2,315,739 vehicles.
- XM (1989-2000) 332,537 vehicles.
- Xantia (1993) 1,178,441 vehicles manufactured (end of 2000).
- Xsara (1997) 714,802 vehicles (end of 2000).
- C5 launched in September 2000, marketed in March 2001.
- Peugeot 407 launched early December 2003, marketed in April 2004.

Condate

Rennes is 2,000 years old – a lesson learnt at the superb exhibition entitled 'Fondations' (Foundations), which took place in spring, 2000 at the Musée de Bretagne. Condate ('confluence' in the Gaulish language) was born where two rivers, the Ille and the Vilaine, meet, and present archaeological knowledge indicates that the Romans were entirely responsible for the city's foundation. The heart of this first city was situated in the area of the cathedral, whereas archaeological excavations elsewhere have revealed important Gaulish rural settlements of an earlier date throughout the Rennes basin. Condate later became 'Civitas Riedones', the city of the Riedones, which in turn produced the name, Rennes.

« Asterix and Latraviata », the latest in the famous comic book series, which takes place partly in Condate, was launched in Rennes on 1 February, 2001. (Uderzo did this drawing especially for the occasion).

C

The 'Coucou de Rennes', a breed of poultry which was on the verge of extinction.

Coucou

As well as being a good layer and a good broody hen, the Coucou de Rennes hen is also famous for the high quality of its meat. It was very nearly a case of 'was famous' because this hardy local breed, once a common sight in the farmyard, was within a hair's breadth of dying out. Its rescue was due to the efforts of the Ecomusée du Pays de Rennes (Rennes Museum of Rural Life), which in 1988 traced the very last specimens to the Angers region, where they were being kept by a former farmer from Rennes, who was an enthusiast of the breed. Today, a producers' association has once again given pride of place to this succulent chicken, which is to be found on the stalls of certain local markets and on the tables of the region's greatest restaurants. The next stage is to be the obtaining of an A.O.C. (Appellation d'Origine Contrôlée), a system of quality control.

(Cultes) Religions

Catholics form the great majority with about 20 churches within the city itself, along with 33 religious communities. The Islamic faith has 8,000 worshippers, according to the Islamic Cultural Centre, while the presence of Buddhism, with about 1,500 worshippers, is due to the Cambodian, Laotian, Vietnamese, Japanese, and Tibetan communities. The Protestants of the French Reformed Church represent about 270 families, not to mention those who attend the Evangelical Church and 'Vie et Lumière' (Life and Light), which is the evangelical mission to the gypsy community. About 100 people attend the Constantinople Orthodox Church, and there is also a French Orthodox Church. The Jewish community, with about 100 families, has had a synagogue since September, 2001.

The Islamic Cultural Centre.

(Deux cent douze mille) Two hundred and twelve thousand

Or more precisely **212,494**, according to the 1999 census. This figure is the population of Rennes, and makes the Breton capital the 10th largest city in France. A particular characteristic of Rennes' population is its youth, with almost 21% being under 20 years of age, and 62% under 40. There are 50,000 schoolchildren and 58,000 students in further and higher education. When the population of all the 36 towns and villages that make up the Rennes Métropole administrative district is taken into account, the population rises to 375,569.

Diwan and Div Yezh

The revival of Breton in the primary school.

Even if Breton has never actually been spoken in Rennes, **the Celtic language has always met with a certain degree of success in the capital.** Interest in it has been growing over a number of years, a fact demonstrated by the increasing number of primary school children attending Breton classes, whether using the bilingual system offered by Div Yezh within state schools, or the intensive method promoted by Diwan.

Dreyfus (Alfred)

August, 1899. Rennes, a perfectly ordinary small city of 70,000 people, was getting ready to experience an event of worldwide importance, **the second Dreyfus trial.** Several weeks earlier, the Cour de Cassation, France's highest Court of Appeal, had referred Captain Alfred Dreyfus, already found guilty of spying for Germany and duly sentenced in 1894, to appear before a court-martial in the Breton capital, a garrison town well-known for its peace and quiet. The trial was to last a month under the eyes of the world's press, with more than 200 journalists, including those from the U.S.A., Russia, Sweden, Turkey, and Argentina, making the journey to Rennes. Most of Rennes' inhabitants were hostile or, at best, indifferent to the accused, and only a very few expressed their support of Dreyfus' case. Their leaders were university academics, from among whom emerged the figure of Victor Basch, and their action was to give birth to the Rennes section of the 'Ligue des Droits de l'Homme' (League of the Rights of Man). Following a month-long hearing, Dreyfus was again found guilty on 9 September, but was pardoned on 19 September by the French President. However, this second judgement was not quashed, and hence Dreyfus' name not cleared, until 1906.

Dreyfus' second trial took place in Rennes in August, 1899.

(Eau) Water

△ **Barges at the Quai Saint-Cyr.** D. Levasseur.

△ **An arm of the river Vilaine in Saint-Hélier.** R. Volante.

△ **The fountain at the Pont de la Mission.** D. Levasseur.

△ **The fountain by Jean-Yves Brélivet in the Francisco Ferrer-Vern area.** R. Volante.

△ **The Ille-and-Rance Canal.** D. Levasseur.

◁ **A fountain in the Place de Bretagne ('The rather unacademic bathers' by Gérard Collin-Thiébaut, 2000).**
D. Levasseur.

△ **The fountain by Claudio Parmiggianni in the Place Coëtquen.**
D. Levasseur.

△ **The fountain in the Place Hoche.**
D. Levasseur.

The old wash-house, Boulevard de Chézy. D. Levasseur.

▷ **The Thabor gardens.** D. Levasseur.

M. Ogier

D. Levasseur.

M. Auger

D. Levasseur.

E.N.S.P., E.N.S.A.R., et al.

At the summit of the French higher education system are the many 'grandes écoles'(specialist universities). Here is a non-exhaustive list of the **'grandes écoles' in the Rennes area:**

• Agriculture: Ecole Nationale Supérieure Agronomique, Institut National Supérieur de Formation Agro-Alimentaire (food processing), Institut d'Etudes Supérieures d'Industrie et d'Economie Laitières (dairy farming)

• Science and technology: Ecole Nationale Supérieure de Chimie (chemistry), Institut National des Sciences Appliquées (applied science), Supélec (Ecole Supérieure d'Electicité) (electronic engineering), Ecole d'Ingénieurs 'Louis de Broglie' (engineering), Ecole Nationale de la Statistique et de l'Analyse de l'Information (statistics and information analysis), Ecole des Métiers de l'Environnement (environment), Institut de Formation Supérieure en Informatique et Communication (data analysis and communication)

• Telecommunications: Ecole Nationale Supérieure des Télécommunications, Ecole Nationale Supérieure de l'Application des Transmissions (an army establishment)

• Health: Ecole Nationale de la Santé Publique (public health)

• Politics: Institut d'Etudes Politiques

• Business: Sup de Co (Rennes Business School), Institut des Hautes Etudes Comptables et Financières (accountancy and finance)

• Education: Ecole Normale Supérieure de Cachan (civil service), Institut Universitaire de Formation des Maîtres (teacher training)

• Arts: Ecole Régionale des Beaux Arts (art), Conservatoire National de la Région (music), Institut Supérieur des Arts Appliqués (applied arts), Ecole du Théâtre National de Bretagne (drama).

D. Levas

D. Levasseur.

February, 1994: the fire at the Parlement de Bretagne.

(Feu) Fires

July, 1911: the fire at the Palais de Commerce.

"Nothing but fire takes hold or catches on in Rennes!", famously remarked a 19th century Archbishop of Rennes, Monseigneur Brossay-Saint-Marc. Fortunately, the city has since woken up and become distinctly livelier, but as far as fires are concerned, its history has certainly been eventful, flames having punctuated every period of its past. There was the great fire of 1720, which raged for 6 days, devastated part of the medieval centre, and so indirectly gave rise to the classical architecture of the rebuilt city centre. Memories of the fire that struck the Parlement de Bretagne (Brittany Parliament) in 1994 remain very strong, but it must not be forgotten that practically all of Rennes' important public buildings have been affected in the past: the Hôpital Saint-Méen (1814), the Opéra (1856), the Ecole Normale des Garçons (1908), the Palais du Commerce (today's Post Office and France Télécom) (1911), the Hôtel de Ville (1920), the Palais Saint-Georges (1921), the Omnia Pathé cinema (1931), the Grand Séminaire (1968), and the School of Dentistry (1975), as well as all the fires that have hit Rennes' businesses, such as the Saint-Hélier Mills in 1934, Lambert's, on the Mail, in 1947, the Oberthür printing works in 1949, Verry's, in the Rue de la Mabilais, in 1957, and Besnard's in the Rue Duhamel, in 1969.

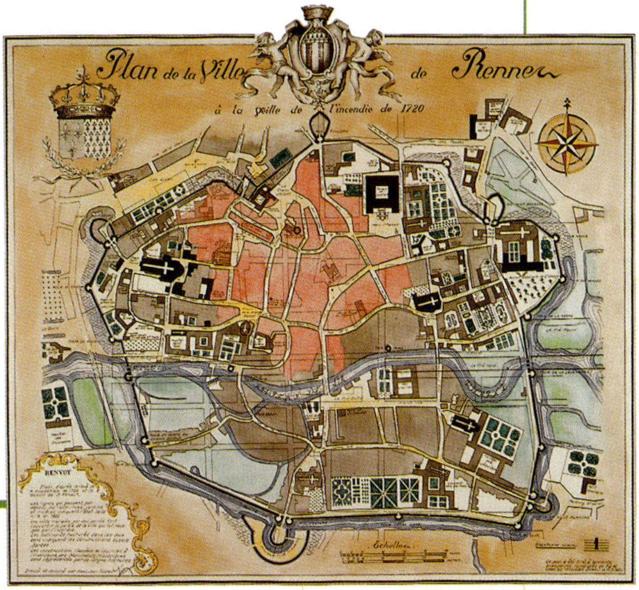

A map of the city just before the 1720 fire. The part destroyed by the fire is marked in red.

F

The author of « Le Bossu » (The Hunchback).

Féval (Paul-Henri)

Paul-Henri Féval the author of *Le Bossu* (The Hunchback), *Les Habits Noirs* (The Black Habits), *La Vampire*, and *Les Mystères de Londres* (The London Mysteries), was considered the equal of Alexandre Dumas the elder. Although born in Rennes, he always kept a certain distance that could euphemistically be described as critical with regard to his home town. In fact, with the sole exception of the Hôtel de Ville ("original, if not grandiose"), no other building found favour with him. The Opéra was "a sad rotunda which was enough to spoil the city centre", whilst as for the Parlement de Bretagne, "The building needed to be enhanced, but they have diminished it. Exactly the sort of thing that they would do."

Fibre Optics

In Rennes, **fibre optics** make up the heart of the new cable network of about 3,000 kilometres, the subscribers being linked by means of copper wire. Fibre optics are also usually used in telecommunication transmission networks. This extremely thin flexible glass strand is highly suited to the transport of signals of light, and also withstands outside interference, making very high speed and high capacity transmissions possible.

Cable television, transmitted by fibre optics, was launched in Rennes in March, 1987.

Fournier (Jean-Claude)

As the creative father of the comic book character, Bizu, and the spiritual son of the comic book artist, Franquin, whose adventures of Spirou he took up again in 1968, Jean-Claude Fournier started a Breton comic book movement in the early 1970s. Once established in Rennes, he opened the doors of his studio to numerous young artists, such as Malo Louarn, Gégé, and Bélom, of whom some, several years later in 1982, launched a bimonthly magazine called 'Frilouz', which marked a milestone in the history of the Breton comic book. 8 issues of 12,000 copies each were published, and brought new talent to light, being where Michel Plessix, the creator of Julien Boisvert and *Le Vent dans les Saules* (The Wind in the Willows) as well as Jean-Luc Hiettre (*Le Grand Fleuve* - The Big River) published their first illustrations. Comic book fanzines took over, one of the most important being 'Atchoum' which successfully managed to launch almost all its authors, e.g. Chauvel, Le Saëc, and Duval, onto the professional market. This dynamism was a breath of fresh air, leading to several artists and writers setting themselves up on the banks of the river Vilaine. Today, there are over 30 of them, including Le Tendre, Andréas, and Sorel, in Rennes and the surrounding area.

The Hôtel de Ville is a very fine example of Gabriel's architecture.

Gabriel

Rennes' classical-style centre owes much to **this family of royal architects** who supervised the city's reconstruction after the great fire of 1720. Jacques-Jules Gabriel (1667 – 1742), and his son, Jacques-Ange (1698 – 1782) succeeded each other at this enormous building site. The Place du Parlement as well as the Hôtel de Ville and its square are their work.

Galette-saucisse

A 'galette-saucisse'- the Breton hot-dog - is **a savoury buckwheat pancake wrapped around a hot sausage,** and is an essential part of the local heritage, being unquestionably one of Ille-et-Vilaine's most distinctive hallmarks. This tasty partnership is to be found at any festival here, and its delicious smell traditionally pervades the evenings of football matches at the Route de Lorient stadium, the home of Rennes' first division football team, the Stade Rennais. The 'galette-saucisse' has its own specialists and places dedicated to its enjoyment, as well as a 'Save the Galette-Saucisse' organisation and a website.

Gallo

Brittany has two languages, Breton and Gallo. Gallo is spoken in Haute-Bretagne (Upper Brittany), particularly in the Rennes area, where Breton has never been spoken, and is not a patois but a Romance dialect derived, like French, from Latin. It now has a modest presence at secondary school and university level, and is enjoying a fresh burst of vitality, largely due to the popularity of Gallo storytellers, but its appearance in print is proving to be somewhat trickier. However, Rue des Scribes, a Rennes-based publisher, has had the good idea of translating three of the adventures of Tintin into Gallo, so lovers of this delightful dialect will be able to enjoy « Sus l'Île Naire » (L'Ile Noire – Black Island), « Les Dorûres à la Castafiore » (Les bijoux de la Castafiore – The Castafiore Jewels), and « La Cutrie dla Licône » (Le Secret de la Licorne -The Secret of the Unicorn).

gG

Génopole Ouest

The sea (marine genetics), **health** (proteins and their functions, genetic therapy), and **food processing** are the three fields of excellence at Génopole Ouest, in which 48 laboratories at INSERM, INRA, CNRS, IFREMER, and the universities participate, with 2,000 researchers at Rennes, Nantes, Angers, Roscoff, and Brest.

This genetics research project is supported by the regional councils of Brittany and the Pays de la Loire, and after scientific assessment in 2001 was granted the title of a national Génopôle, like similar centres at Strasbourg, Lyons-Grenoble, Lille, Toulouse, Montpellier, Evry, and Aix-Marseilles.

Goncourt

The announcement of the award at the La Chope restaurant. Here, in November, 2000, the secondary school students chose « Allah n'est pas obligé » (Allah is not obliged) by Ahmadou Kourama.

Rennes has its own Prix Goncourt, a literary prize which has become almost as famous as that awarded by the Académie Goncourt. Since 1988, on the combined initiative of the 'Bruit de Lire' (Crazy about Reading) organisation, the Ministry of Education, and FNAC, the French multi-media chain, a jury of sixth-form students has announced its own choice, on the same day as the Académie, live from the La Chope restaurant. The selection for the prize initially involved only the young people of Rennes, but now final year students from all over France (and even from abroad) take part, and this led to the creation of the Rencontres Goncourt in 1991, during which authors meet and talk face-to-face with their young readers.

Rennes has yet another link with the Prix Goncourt, albeit more remote, as in 1949, Robert Merle, a Rennes University lecturer, was awarded the prize for his novel, *Week-end à Zuydcoote.*

Haemochromatosis

Like cystic fibrosis, **haemochromatosis is particularly widespread in Brittany,** where 1 person in 200 is affected (compared to the national average of 1 in 300). This fact explains the presence at Rennes' main hospital, the CHRU-Pontchaillou, of France's most highly specialised screening centre. This genetic disease is characterised by excessive iron in the body, and is typified, from the age of 30-35 years onwards, by general fatigue and a tanned complexion, frequently accompanied by an enlarged cirrhotic liver, diabetes, or an irregular heartbeat.

(Bronze diabetes)

(Inondations) Floods

The Vélodrome area was completely inundated during the 1966 floods.

Rennes' dramatic history swings between water and fire. The oldest flood recorded in the city archives dates from January, 1881. Mention can also be found of more localised floods, such as those of the river Ille which affected the mills in Rennes in July, 1809. In October, 1966, small boats were used to cross the Rue Saint-Hélier, and the Alphonse-Guérin cycling track was transformed into a huge swimming pool, as was the Avenue Aristide Briand and the town of Cesson-Sévigné. In November, 1974, floods affected 436 residents, businesses, and farmers. In May, 1981, the jamming of the Saint-Martin lock gates caused flooding that led to the evacuation of 150 local residents. Since then, a huge investment has been made in flood prevention and protection measures, most notably with the construction of pumping stations, and this has meant that Rennes has largely been spared during the most recent floods of 1995, 1999, 2000, and 2001 which have hit Ille-et-Vilaine one after another.

Under the fountain on the Quai Aristide Briand is one of the pumping stations that has been constructed as a flood prevention measure.

(Jumelles (villes)) Twin cities

Rennes is twinned with 11 cities and 1 region:

1957: Exeter (United Kingdom)
1958: Rochester (USA)
1964: Erlangen (Germany)
1965: Brno (Czech Republic)
1967: Sendai (Japan)
1980: Leuven (Louvain) (Belgium)
1982: Sétif (Algeria)
1983: Cork (Ireland)
1991: Almaty (Kazakhstan)
1998: Poznan (Poland)
1999: Sibiu (Rumania)
2001: Dogon Plateau (Mali)

△ **Leuven.** Ville de Rennes (direction de l'information).

△ **Pozňan.** I. Audigé.

◁ **Jinan.** M.-F. Kerroc'h.

▽ **Almaty.** J.-P. Roullier.

▽ **The Dogon Plateau.** Ville de Rennes (direction de l'information).

▽ **Erlangen.** M. Festoc.

△ **Sibiu.** D. Levasseur. △ **Rochester.** D.R. ▽ **Cork.** F. Trouilloud.

△ **Sétif.** G. Prudor. ▷ **Sendai.** D.R.

△ **Brno.** J.-P. Roullier. ▽ **Exeter.** Desclos.

J

Jazy (Michel)

It was during the heyday of the highly popular athletics meetings at the Courtemanche stadium that **Michel Jazy** presented the people of Rennes with two records. On 9 June, 1965, he beat the world record for the mile (1,609 metres) in 3 minutes 53.6 seconds. A year later, on 15 June, 1966, he set a new French record of 3 minutes 36.4 seconds for the 1500 metres.

The 'Rennes' rose, created by Michel Adam.

Jenny

« Grand-mère Jenny » is one of the 981 varieties of roses in the Thabor's rose garden. A tribute paid by a nurseryman to his grandmother, it modestly rubs shoulders with the princesses Caroline of Monaco and Margaret of England, Romy Schneider, Josephine Baker, Sylvie Vartan, Charles de Gaulle, Honoré de Balzac, Christian Dior, and the French comic actor, Louis de Funès.

Other roses were named after a town, city, or business, or else according to the wishes of their creators, or their customers. Among such roses can be found some beautifully original names, such as 'Nuage Parfumée' (Perfumed Cloud), 'Idylle', 'Bébé Lune (Baby Moon), 'Blue Girl', 'Caprice', and 'Sourire d'Enfant' (Child's Smile). Rennes also has its own rose, created by Michel Adam, a local rose-breeder.

The roses in the Thabor are divided into several sections – climbing and weeping roses, a patch for new breeds, a circular rose garden, and a garden of old roses. Among these latter are the white rose of York and Lancaster, created in 1551, as well as 'Cuisse de Nymphe' (Nymph's Thigh), created in 1797, 'Madame Plantier', created in 1835, and, from 1890, 'Rosa Sericea Pteracantha', with its translucent thorns.

Langlais (Xavier de)

A teacher at Rennes' Ecole de Beaux Arts (school of art) for 25 years, Xavier de Langlais is the author of *La Technique de la Peinture à l'Huile de Van Eyck à Nos Jours* (Oil-painting Technique from Van Eyck to the Present-day), which continues to be the definitive work on the subject, with 30 reprints since 1959 and numerous translations, including Japanese. In addition to this important publication on the subject of art, his literary output has also been significant, including plays and novels, including *L'Ile sous Cloche* (The Island under Glass), published by Editions Présence du Futur, and, in particular, his translations of the Arthurian legend in Breton and French, sometimes illustrated with his own woodcuts.

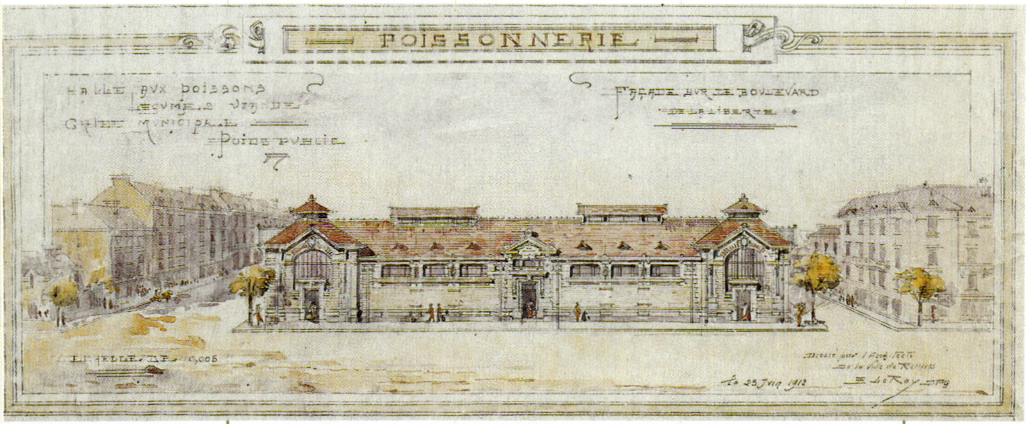

Here, one of Le Ray's watercolours illustrates his plan for the Halles (indoor market) on the Boulevard de la Liberté

Le Ray (Emmanuel)

Emmanuel Le Ray worked with seven successive mayors of Rennes from 1895 to 1932, most notably with Jean Javier (1908 – 1923), when he constructed many public buildings in Rennes. **As the municipal architect,** he designed an impressive number of buildings, from schools, nurseries, public baths and bathhouses, market halls, war memorials, and funeral chapels to private houses and shops. Le Ray's work is absolutely everywhere in the city, whether the Piscine Saint-Georges (public baths), the Halles Centrales (indoor market), the Lycée Robidou (school), the Palais de Commerce (now the Post Office and French Télécom), the Galeries Lafayette department store, or the Magasins Modernes (now the Virgin Megastore). In addition to his talents as an architect, he was also a gifted watercolour artist, as is shown by this 1912 plan depicting the future Halle aux Poissons (Fish Market) in the Boulevard de la Liberté.

The city architect's long career has left its mark in the city centre.

Lices

This large Saturday morning market is an essential meeting-place for the people of Rennes.

If you have never been to **the market in the Place des Lices,** you most certainly have not seen all the city. You must experience at least once this weekly rendezvous which is held on the spot where, or so it is said, Bertrand Du Guesclin, the famous Breton warrior, broke a few lances at the jousts at the foot of the walls of the medieval city. This extremely colourful and aromatic Saturday morning ritual is an essential port of call both for the region's great restaurateurs and for leaflet distributors, as well as being everyone's favourite meeting-place. For those who are allergic to the city centre, Rennes also has local markets, such as those of Sainte-Thérèse, Villejean, or Zagreb, which are just as colourful and welcoming.

(Marocains) Moroccans

The Moroccans, with their 1,947 nationals (*Prefectural statistics, 2000*), make up **Rennes' largest foreign community,** followed by the Turks (1,074), Germans (919), Portuguese (899), British (895), Spanish (739), Algerians (704), and Americans (568). 15,315 foreigners, i.e. a little more than 7% of the population, live in the Breton capital, and among the 150 countries thus represented, sometimes by a single national, are Mongolia, Zimbabwe, Saint Lucia, Latvia, Surinam, Tadzhikistan, Costa Rica, and Fiji.

Martin

According to the telephone directory, **Martin is the most common surname in Rennes,** the Breton capital thereby conforming statistically to the national situation. This fact is further emphasised by the appearance after Martin of other surnames that come from first names, such as Gautier (and Gaulthier), Thomas, Simon, and Hervé. A truly local name does not appear until sixth place with the not entirely unexpected Lebreton and Le Breton.

Melaine

This early 6th century **saint-bishop of Rennes** has both a street and a church named after him. In *Contes et Légendes de Haute Bretagne* (Tales and Legends of Upper Brittany), Albert Poulain tells how at the saint's death, the people of Redon and Rennes quarrelled about who was to have his remains. In order to reach a decision and so end to the dispute, the body was put on a small boat, which was then pushed out into the river. The boat miraculously actually floated upstream along the Vilaine to Rennes, where the saint's body was embalmed and laid in a shrine within the cathedral.

The church of Notre-Dame-en-Saint-Melaine stands on the Thabor hill.

Metro

Rennes' metro (underground transport system) **is a VAL** (véhicule automatique léger – automatic light vehicle), which has been developed by Matra Transport International. Line A runs over a total distance of 9.4 kilometres, and serves 15 stations in about 16 minutes along a south-east/north-west axis that runs through the historic city centre. Construction work was started in January, 1997, and lasted five years, with the metro becoming fully operational in March, 2002. The total cost of this undertaking was 449 million euros (2,942 million francs - at the 1995 value).

Since it opened in March, 2002, Rennes' new transport system has been an overwhelming success. (78,700 pasengers on 28 March, 2002, for example).

Monuments and architecture

△ **The Opera House.**
D. Levasseur.

◁ **Place des Lices.**
R. Volante.

▽ **Church of Saint-Sauveur.**
D. Levasseur.

△ **Place du Parlement.** R. Volante.

▽ **Rue du Chapitre.** D. Levasseur.

△ **Rue Motte-Fablet.** D. Levasseur.

▽ **Palais Saint-Georges.** D. Levasseur.

▷ **Halle Martenot (covered market)** D. Levasseur.

Monuments and architecture

▽ **Rue Saint-Georges.**
R. Volante.

◁◁ **Piscine Saint-Georges (swimming pool)**
D. Levasseur.

◁ **Place Hoche.**
R. Volante.

△ **Hôtel des Ventes (auction room), Place des Lices.**
D. Levasseur.

▽ **Church of Vieux-Saint-Etienne**
R. Volante.

△ **The towers of 'Les Horizons' flats** R. Volante.

▽ **The Station.** D. Levasseur. △ **Place Sainte-Anne.** D. Levasseur.
▷ **The Opera House** D. Levasseur.

▽ **Rue de Brest.** R. Volante. ▽ **The Station.** D. Levasseur. △ **Barre Saint-Just.** D. Levasseur.
▽ **Place Sainte-Anne.** D. Levasseur.

M

Métropole

The ***Hôtel de la communauté d'agglomération*****, designed by architects Patrick Berger and Jacques Anziutti and located on the ZAC Clemenceau site, is home to the Metropolitan District's elected officials and departments.**

Photo credit: Model T. Martin, photo M. Paslier.

Rennes Métropole was born on 1 January, 2000. 36 towns and villages, together representing some 365,000 people, joined forces in a single administrative unit to deal with those responsibilities common to all areas of local authority cooperation, such as economic development, higher education and research, housing development, public transport, the environment, waste disposal, the funding of cultural and sporting facilities, and highways and parking.

This inter-local authority cooperation had already had a long history as Rennes District was formed in 1970, and, from 1992 onwards, was the first French local authority to vote for a single business tax. Rennes Métropole continues to pursue and develop this dynamic form of cooperation.

METROPOLE Rennes vivre en intelligence

Minitel

This famous little screen was created in the late 1970s **in the Rennes laboratories of the C.C.E.T.T.** (Centre Commun d'Etudes de Télédiffusion et Télécommunication), which is today the Research and Development section of France Télécom. It first underwent tests in the Saint-Malo region in 1980, and then in the homes of 300,000 subscribers in Ille-et-Vilaine during 1981-82, being marketed in the whole of France in 1983. However, with the arrival of the Internet, this Rennes 'baby' is looking distinctly old-fashioned.

Motte-Picquet (La)

Toussaint-Guillaume Picquet de La Motte was born in Rennes in 1720. He was a famous sailor, renowned for his tactical skills, who distinguished himself during the American War of Independence, dying at Brest at the age of 71, after 52 years of service!

Several ships of the French navy have been named after him, the latest of which is an anti-submarine frigate which was launched in 1985. This ship forms part of the Force d'Action Navale (Naval Action Force), and has been sponsored by the City of Rennes since 1987.

(Millième) A Thousandth

On the Dogon Plateau, Mali.

Since 1985, Rennes City Council has allocated an annual sum equivalent to 1/1,000 of its budget to **the financing of Third World development projects.** Mali's Dogon Plateau and the Hué region of Vietnam are among the places that benefit from the activities involved in this decentralised cooperation, activities which, once set up, are always run by local people.

N.T.I.C.

In Rennes, the **Nouvelles Technologies de l'Information et de la Communication** are not really new at all as the Rennes Atalante Beaulieu Science & Technology Park has long been recognised as a European telecommunications centre. There are 56 research laboratories, including 38% in the IT sector, working in the fields of mobile telephony, telecommunication services, digital TV and multimedia. 5,200 students (out of a total of 58,500) follow courses in these fields.

(Nouveau-né) The Newborn

Georges de la Tour's (1593 - 1652) famous painting, was, for a long time, attributed to the Le Nain brothers, and is a sort of emblem for Rennes' Musée de Beaux-Arts (art gallery). The Musée de Beaux Arts is itself renowned for the wealth of its collections of 17th century paintings, which were particularly admired in the memorable 'Grand Siècle' exhibition in 1993. However, this particular area of specialisation should not mean that the full range of the museum's reserve collections should be overlooked. These include most notably a superb collection of over a thousand Italian drawings, in addition to sculptures and numerous other works of art.

O

The former Oberthür printing works in the Rue de Paris closed its doors in 1983. This superb industrial building has been converted into a business centre.

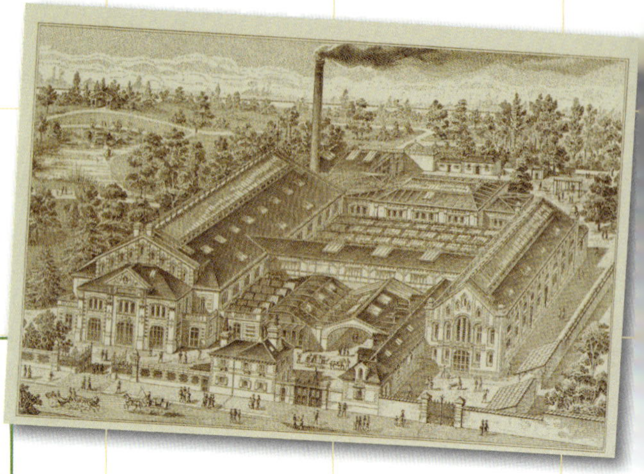

Oberthur

In the south-eastern industrial estate is to be found one of the two fiduciary printing divisions of the **François-Charles Oberthur group,** named after the famous 19th century Rennes printer, the second being located in North Carolina. Here is printed the currency for 45 countries, as well as passports, identity cards, visas, title-deeds, certificates, and other documents denoting value and security. Created in 1984, the François-Charles Oberthür fiduciary group spearheads the group which lies in third place worldwide with regards to private fiduciary printers. This international group also prints lottery tickets, credit cards, and secured cheques.

Odorico

The Odoricos were an Italian family who came to live in Rennes in the late 19th century. They brought with them **the elegance and colour of mosaic art,** which was then unknown in Brittany, and of which many examples remain in the city, with just as many decorating the facades of buildings as their interiors.

Où il fait bon vivre...

In 1995, Rennes was named the best town to live in by the French magazine *Ça m'intéresse*. It was awarded the same title the following year and again in 1999 (by the magazine *Testé pour vous cette fois*). In January 2003, it came runner up in the "France's best towns to live in" competition, run by *Le Point* magazine. Four titles from an impressive list of awards accumulated since the 1980s. Rennes was recently recognised for its initiatives for women (March 2000), student facilities (November 1999), public area planning (2000, 2002), its initiatives in new technology (2001, 2002) and sporting events (2003, *L'Expansion*), and it recently came top for its economic dynamism (2004, *L'Express*).

« Ouest-France »

France's leading newspaper is published in... Rennes. « Ouest-France » was created in August, 1944, following on from its predecessor, « L'Ouest-Éclair », and with daily sales of almost 800,000, it has the largest circulation among France's 'dailies'. Its large number of local editions cover the 12 departments of the Greater West, making 'the paper', as many of its readers call it, an essential part of local life.

P p

Palets

This is played with pieces of flat, round metal (a sort of flattened form of 'boules'), and is **Upper Brittany's traditional game 'par excellence',** being played here on a board. There are even, from time to time, French championships of the game, but competitors rarely come from further away than Mayenne, the next department! The playing of palets is very much alive, and takes place in farmyards or in the backyards of cafés in Rennes. The game has even been known to have been packed up in a luggage hold to be played on holiday abroad!

Palets are part of the local tradition, just like cider and 'galette saucisses'.

Pantheon

One of Rennes' treasures is unique in France. After the First World War, the city, led by its mayor, Jean Janvier, wanted to honour its dead, but not simply by erecting a traditional war memorial. It was decided that a room in the town hall should be dedicated to their memory, and so, using bronze, Italian marble, and carefully conceived lighting, great care was lavished on this unique monument which was inaugurated in 1922, and which attracted the attention of the whole of France. The Rennes painter, Camille Godet, was given the task of creating a wall-painting depicting life in the trenches, and it is here that the faces of the people of Rennes alive at that period can be seen together with such famous figures as Clemenceau and Poincaré. The names of about a thousand dead, from the First World War as well as from later conflicts, are carved on 26 marble slabs. The names of great French generals appear on the ceiling, but Pétain's name has been concealed under a piece of cardboard since 1944!

Part of the fresco by Camile Godet inside the Hôtel de Ville.

Papier Timbré (Revolt)

The Papier Timbré Revolt rocked Rennes in spring, 1675. It was ostensibly a reaction against the many taxes, especially those on administrative acts and legal documents (from whence the name 'papier timbré' – stamped paper), introduced by Louis XIV in order to finance his wars. The city's inhabitants destroyed the tax collectors' offices, but the riot also led to the loss of life. The revolt moved away from Rennes, gained ground in many other Breton towns, and had its rural counterpart in Finistère under the name of the 'Révolte des Bonnets Rouges' (Revolt of the Red Hats). Repression of the revolt was very harsh, with the Duc de Chaulnes, Brittany's governor, ordering about ten executions, fines, and the destruction of part of the Rue Haute (the present Rue Saint-Malo), from which the residents were driven away, as is shown in this illustration from the school textbook, *Histoire de France,* by Ernest Lavisse. The revolt also marked the Brittany Parliament's exile in Vannes until 1690, when it finally returned to Rennes.

Two pictures of the repression that followed the Breton uprisings against royal power in 1675 : an allegorical painting by J. Chalette depicting the 'unjustly suppressed' Bretons, and a realistic drawing showing the people of Rennes being driven out of their city (from « Histoire de France », a primary school textbook by Ernest Lavisse.

Map of Rennes

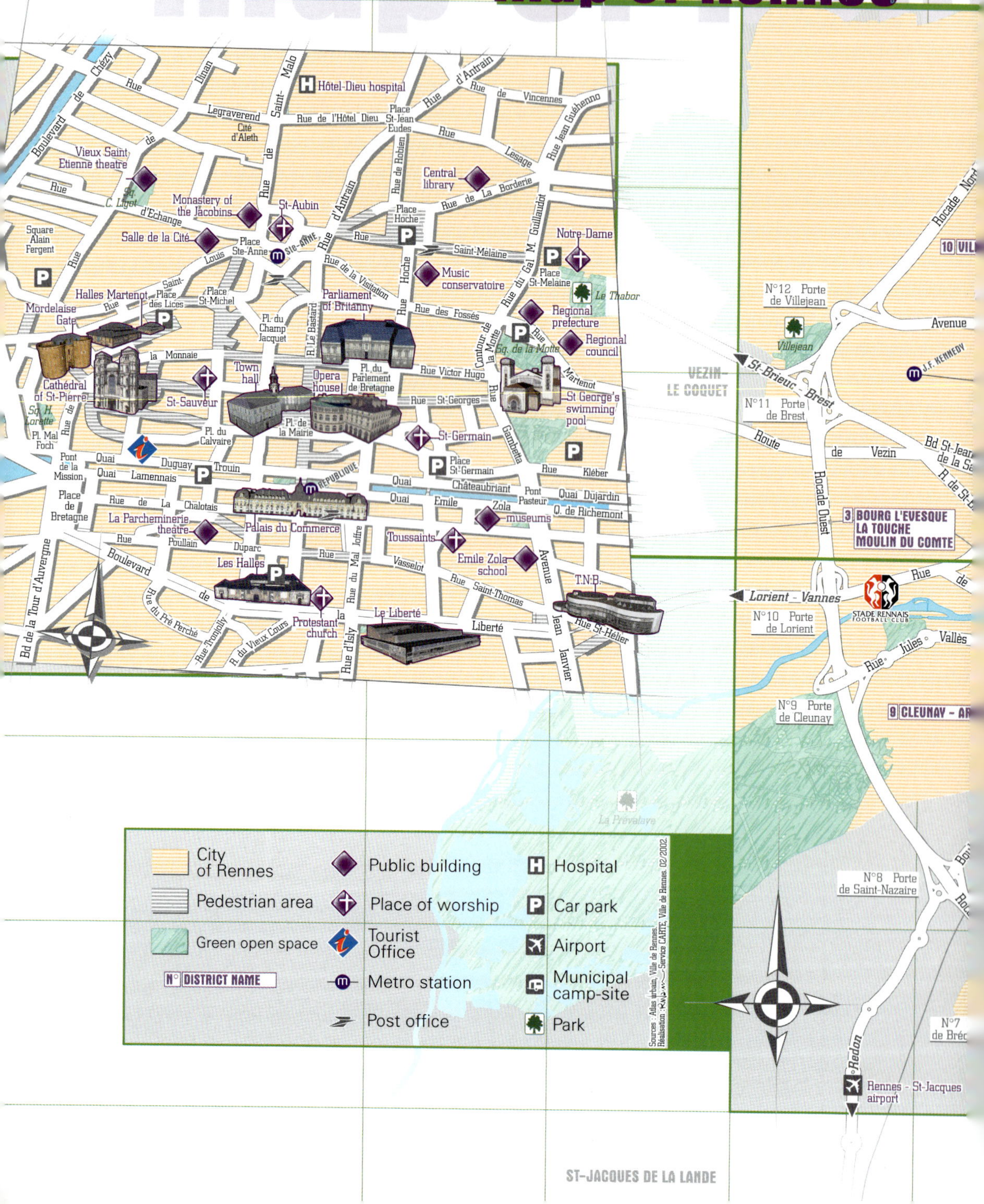

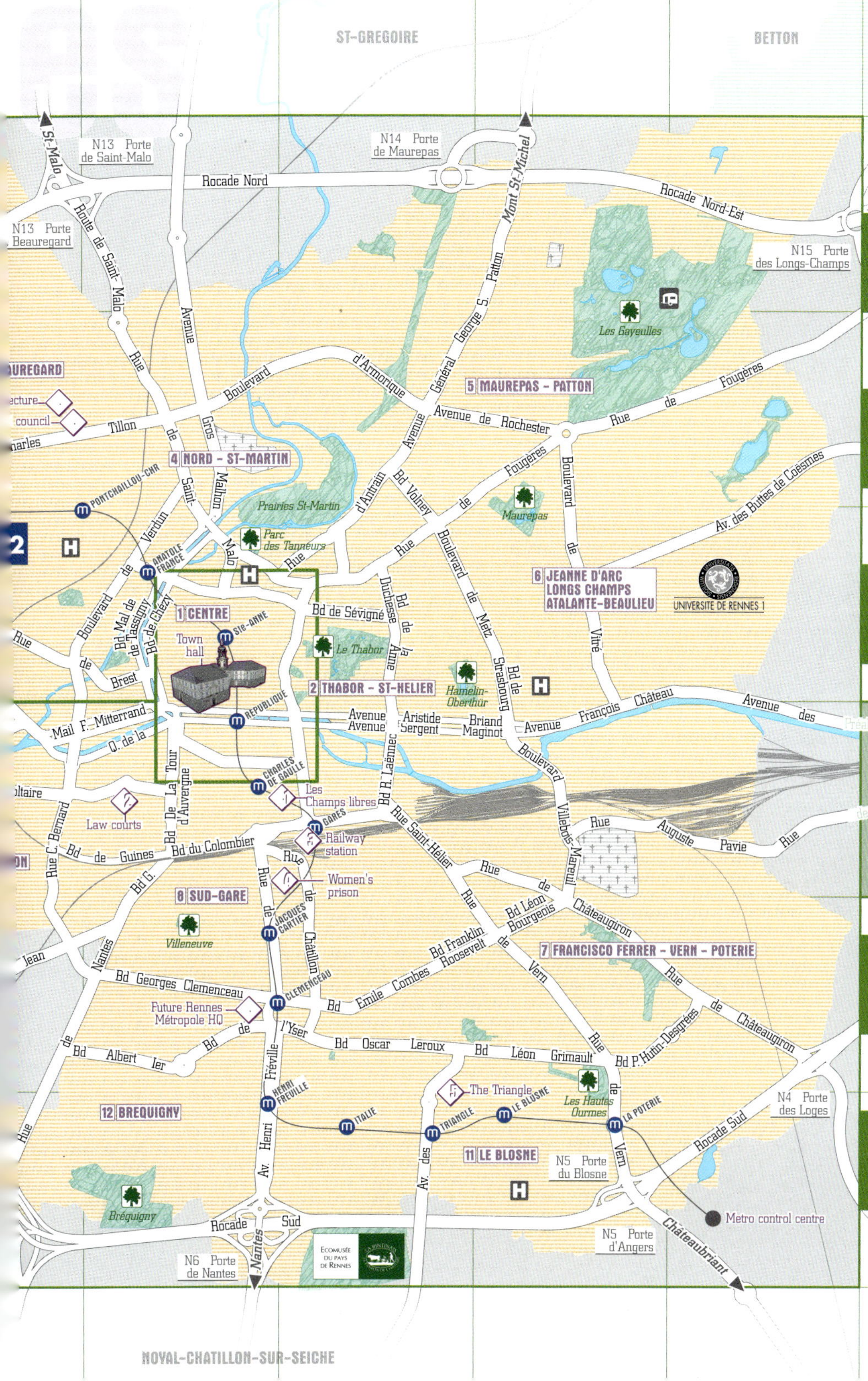

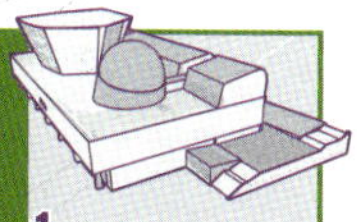
1 Les Champs libres

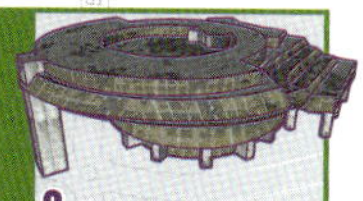
2 Law courts

3 Railway station

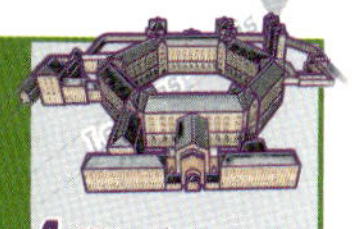
4 Women's prison

5 The Triangle

Pp

The seat of the Court of Appeal.

Parliament

During the night of the fire of 4 and 5 February, 1994, a great many of Rennes' inhabitants fully realised the place that this building occupied, not merely in the city's history but also in local hearts. Since the fire, **it has become one of Rennes' most visited monuments.** Constructed between 1618 and 1655 under the supervision of Salomon de Brosse, and later modified during the 18th century by Gabriel, the building, which is an outstanding example of 17th century French style, notably because of its interior decoration, called upon the talents of the most famous artists of the century of Louis XIV. The former seat of the Breton Parliament later became the city's law courts, and now houses the Court of Appeal.

One of the finest examples of 17th century French architectural style, especially with regards to its interior decoration.

The Liberty stones mark the route taken by American troops during the Liberation.

Patton (George)

On 4 August, 1944, Rennes was the first city in France to be liberated and thereby to gain the new political and administrative powers conceived by the Resistance movement. It was the American Third Army that entered Rennes, after being involved in some hard fighting on the city's outskirts, and its commander, General George S. Patton, was made an honorary citizen.
To commemorate the Allied advance, a Voie de la Liberté (Liberty Way) was created on the personal initiative of G. de la Vasselais, the then head of the tactical liaison service attached to the 20th Corps of the Third Army. Starting at Cherbourg, the Voie de la Liberté marks the route taken by the liberating forces by the positioning of posts every kilometre along the way. These posts are 1.2 metres high, weigh 600 kg, and are made of white stone, decorated with the flame of victory and some stars, which are a reminder of the 50 American states. There should be seven of these waymarkers in Rennes, crossing the city from north to south, but the one that used to stand at the corner of the Avenue Patton and Avenue des Monts d'Arrée has now disappeared.

Rennes, place de la Mairie, 4 August, 1944.

(Phoque) Seal

At the end of their tour around Brittany, Gustave Flaubert and Maxime Du Camp, the French writers, arrived in Rennes, where, after dining somewhat frugally on some lamb chops, they went for a walk along the banks of the Vilaine. There, they found a fairground wagon in their way, and a woman persuaded them to visit the fair's seal, which had apparently been captured only after fierce fighting. Flaubert devotes over a page to a detailed description of this particular fairground attraction. The story has a rather nasty punch line: **"This is what we saw in Rennes. When the seal is no longer there, what will there be to see?"**

P p

Pochons (Saint of the)

In the Cimetière du Nord (Northern Cemetery) there is a strange tomb whose occupant, Mme de Coëtlogon, is supposed to cure fevers and, doubtless, lots of other ailments as well. For this to be done, a piece of earth must be removed from the tomb and put into a bag ('pochon'), which should then be hung around the sick person's neck, before the earth is returned to its rightful owner several days later. This strange ritual, of which there are so many in Brittany, originated 200 years ago. In 1798, during the demolition of the Chapelle des Carmes, where the woman had first been buried in 1677, her body had to be transferred to another burial ground. However, it was found that the body was miraculously still intact 120 years later! News quickly spread, and the second tomb became the object of veneration – and so it remains to this day.

A 200-year old practice that is still very much alive today.

A room in Henri Pollès' house in Brunoy (Essonne).

Pollès (Henri)

Henri Pollès was a **writer and enthusiastic book collector** who was born in Tréguier, and who, between 1933 and 1994, amassed some 30,000 books, manuscripts, drawings, and engravings, which he gave to the city of Rennes.

With its first editions, drafts and fragments of works, catalogues, and patchwork bindings and cases decorated according to his own designs, the Pollès collection is a sort of museum of 20th century literature within the public library.

Incidentally, this passion for book collecting proved fatal to him, as he died, at the age of 85, suffocated by a fire in part of his personal library.

(Porte de Bretagne)

"When I go to Brittany, and when I arrive there by road, rather than by train, when I have gone past Rennes, after an hour or thereabouts, I don't know why but I am happy, I am at home, I know who I am, it's my region..."
Eugène Guillevic, *Un brin d'herbe, après tout.*

Gateway (to Brittany)

Argentré's 1618 map of Rennes.

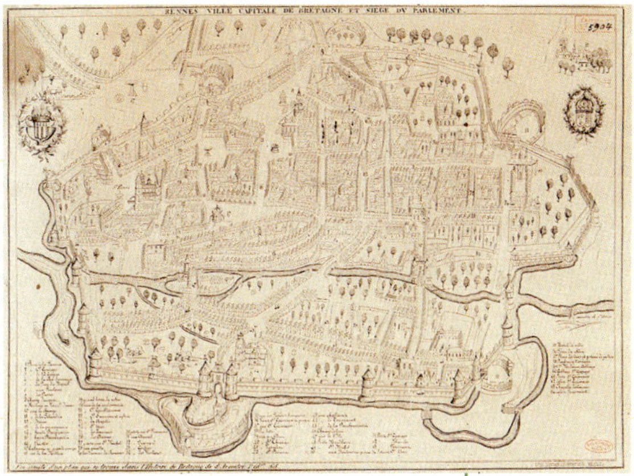

(Portes Mordelaises) Mordelaises Gates

These gates, **the most beautiful remains of Rennes' old city walls,** stand opposite the cathedral. The Mordelaises Gates are also called the Porte Royale as it was here that the Dukes of Brittany and Bishops of Rennes used to make their ceremonial entrance into the city. Along with the Tour du Chêne (Oak Tower) not far away, and some pieces of wall here and there, the gates are one of the rare vestiges of the three sets of walls which encircled Rennes over the centuries. It has to be said that the Rennes city walls had hardly been finished when they very rapidly lost their defensive importance. Their demolition began in the early 16th century, and lasted until the early 20th century.

The former Porte Royale.

The demolition of the Fourgon Tower in 1909 (on the present site of the Quai Duguay-Trouin).

P p

Poterie (metro station)

Reminiscent of a giant butterfly, the Poterie underground station is both imposing and graceful. Like the viaduct, which nimbly straddles the Rennes ring road, the station - which is the first stop on the underground line - is the work of the British architect Sir Norman Foster who also designed the new Reichstag in Berlin.

Over the years, many great architects have left their mark on Rennes, for example Christian de Portzamparc, who designed the Champs Libres, the Cité de la Musique in Paris, the extension of the Palais des Congrès in Paris and the French Embassy in Berlin.

The Poterie metro station and the viaduct that crosses the ring road were designed by the British architect, Sir Norman Foster.

Postuminus

Was Postuminus Rennes' first inhabitant? He was one of the first, in any case, his existence in the 2nd century A.D. being vouched for by an inscribed granite slab that was found during excavations on the Quai Duguay-Trouin in 1968. Titus Flavius Postuminus, who was a priest, is described as a "very honourable citizen."

Sévigné (Marquise de)

With her marriage to Henri de Sévigné, a member of an old Breton aristocratic family, **Marie de Rabutin-Chantal** linked her life as a woman of letters to Brittany, as she wrote almost 300 letters from the Château des Rochers, near Vitré. When in Rennes, however, she liked to mix with 'society', especially that of the governor of Brittany. Disarmingly thoughtless and selfish, she supported the repressive measures taken by the governor of Brittany in order to put down the Papier Timbré revolt. "This province", she wrote in October, 1675, "is in the greatest distress. M. de Chaulnes has taken away the Parlement de Bretagne in order to punish the city ... But I find all this extremely good, as long as the 4,000 soldiers in Rennes do not prevent me from going for walks in the woods, which are remarkably tall and beautiful."

Régnaux

Rennes-les-Bains, our twin sister in the Aude.

The 'Régnaux' are not called 'Rennais', even though they live in Rennes – but in Rennes-sur-Loue in the Doubs department ! There are 90 of them in a small village that nestles in a valley in the Jura mountains, where, despite the presence of a river called La Furieuse, peace and quiet are guaranteed.

At the other end of France, in the Aude, lies Rennes-les-Bains, which, with its 160 inhabitants, or 'Rennois' is twinned with its big sister in Brittany. It is a spa with hot water springs, and lies in the heart of Cathar country in the magnificent landscape of the Corbières. During the 1980s, the modernisation of its spa facilities, of which there is evidence since Roman times, boosted the village's economy.

A few kilometres away, perched on a rocky peak, the village of Rennes-le-Château (111 inhabitants) owes its fame to a priest, the Abbé Saunière, who, in the late 19th century, made his fortune thanks to a 'treasure', the source of which was never revealed, but which still excites people's imaginations.

The last of our Rennes is not far from us, lying on the borders of Maine and Normandy, near Lassay-les-Châteaux. It doubtless owes its highly original name of Rennes-en-Grenouilles (Rennes-in-Frogs) to the fact that in the past its inhabitants, of which there are 105 today, often had their feet in the waters of the nearby river Mayenne.

Rennes (street and metro)

The Rue de Rennes is said to be **the most incomplete street in Paris.** It was opened in 1853 to link Montparnasse station with the banks of the Seine, but comes to a premature end in the Place Saint-Germain-des-Prés, due to the fact of the abandonment of the destruction of private townhouses in the Rue Bonaparte, necessary to clear the way for the Rue de Rennes' continuation, by Baron Haussmann.

The Rue de Rennes also has a metro station of the same name. However, it was closed during the Second World War, did not reopen until June, 1968, and has the fewest passengers of any station on line 12 – 862,000 people started their journeys there in 1999, compared with 7.5 million people at Saint-Lazare! It has to be said, however, that Rennes is only open until 8pm, and is closed on Sundays and public holidays.

Rennes, a little-used station on the Paris metro.

Rennes runs, swims, skates...

△ **Rennes sur Roulettes (roller skates).**
D. Levasseur.

◁ **Tout Rennes Court (running).**
D. Levasseur.

▷ **Fête de Cheval (Horse Show).**
D. Levasseur.

◁ **Grand prix cycliste (cyclin**
D. Levasseur.

▷ **Tout Rennes nage (swimming).** D. Levasseur.

△ **The opening of Le Blizz ice-skating rink.**
H. El Boughammi.

◁ **Triathlon.**
D. Levasseur.

▽ **Tout Rennes marche (walking).**
D. Levasseur.

▷ **Beach volleyball.**
D. Levasseur.

Rr

Rennes 1; a lecture theatre in the Law Department

Rennes 1/Rennes 2

Rennes is a university town and you only need walk around its streets on a Thursday night to realise this. 58,500 students follow higher education courses in the town's many institutes, schools and colleges. The two universities (Rennes I and Rennes II) attract the majority of students. These universities are heirs to the former faculties and date back to the 18th century with the arrival of the Department of Law. Rennes I, the science university, is home to nearly 26,300 students spread over three campuses (Beaulieu, Villejean and the town centre) and Rennes II, the arts university, has 23,466 students on its Villejean campus. These two universities also have campuses in other towns in Brittany.

Rennes 2; the entrance to the Languages Department

(Révolution Française) French Revolution

Did the French Revolution begin in Rennes in January, 1789? The bloody conflict that took place between the nobility and the commoners of the Third Estate could well lay claim to such a fact. Chateaubriand was both a participant in and a witness of this episode. Although he was too young to have voting rights, he was there to assist his noble colleagues:
"The Etats took place in the Jacobins monastery in the Place du Palais. We went into the meeting room, and were no sooner seated than the people besieged us. [...] The Rennes School of Law, at the head of which was Moreau, had gone and fetched the young people of Nantes, of whom 400 arrived, and the commander, in spite of all his entreaties, could not prevent them from invading the city. [...].
Weary of being stuck in our room, we decided to make our way outside, swords in hand. This really was quite a sight to behold. At our president's signal, we all drew our swords at the same time to the cry of "Vive la Bretagne!", and, like a garrison with nothing to lose, we rushed out wildly to attack those besieging us. The people greeted us with screams and howls, the throwing of stones, blows from iron-clad clubs, and pistol shots."

Michel Gérard, who was called Father Gérard, was one of the Rennes representatives, and one of the few farmers, at the Estates -General at Versailles.

The early stirrings of the French Revolution began in January, 1789, when there were clashes between law students and young aristocrats in the Place du Parlement.

(Révolution industrielle) Industrial Revolution

Rennes did not experience the Industrial Revolution. Right up to the years immediately after the Second World War, the city was made up of a mixture of craftsmen, shopkeepers, and civil servants, as well as several protected industries, such as the printing works, the railways, and the arsenal. Rennes' prosperity was due to its institutional rather than to its industrial activities.
The coming of Citroën in 1961 did not really make it a car-manufacturing city. It was the transfer of such 'grandes écoles' as the army's Ecole Nationale Supérieure de l'Application des Transmissions, the Ecole Nationale Supérieure des Télécommunications, and the Ecole Supérieure d'Electricité that laid the foundations for the Rennes region's long-lasting specialisation in computer science and information and communication technology.

rR

Robien (Christophe-Paul de)

Christophe-Paul de Robien (1698-1756) was the sort of archetypal enlightened gentleman who was a driving force in provincial cultural life during the 18th century. He came from an old noble family, was a great landowner, and a prominent member of the Breton Parliament, but he was also a naturalist, geographer, and historian. Passionately fond, as he was, of his native Brittany, he undertook the compilation of a comprehensive encyclopaedia on the region, and to this end he collected thousands of objects and works of art in his Rennes townhouse (which can still be seen at the corner of the Rues Le Bastard and du Champ Jacquet). This extensive collection was confiscated during the Revolution, and made up the first collections of the city's museums and libraries.

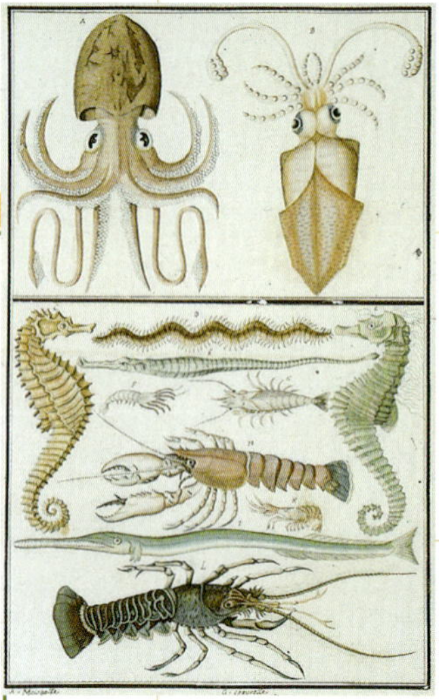

(Rouge et Noir) Red and Black

Red and Black are symbolic of Breton football as they are the colours worn by the top two teams in the region, En-Avant Guingamp and Stade Rennais. Even if you are not a football fan, you should take in the atmosphere in the stadium on the Route de Lorient with its wonderful smell of grilled sausages. This stadium has recently been renovated. The architects Matthieu Lucet and Bruno Gaudin and the French building company GTB worked together for five years to meet the requirements of the French National Football League which stipulates that a French Premiere Division football stadium must hold a minimum of 20,000 people, with enough seating for two thirds of the supporters. Work began on 18 January 1999 and was carried out without disrupting any matches.
Today, Rennes stadium can seat 31,217 people compared with 7,342 in 1998. This handicap did not however prevent this hundred-year-old club from winning the French Cup in 1965 and 1971.

Boutet, Aubour, Prouff, Hiard, Cardiet – the reunion of former players and their trainer during the centenary celebrations in 2001.

Soarès (Mario)

Mario Soares, the then president of Portugal, on a visit to Rennes in 1991.

Mario Soares, the former president of Portugal (1986 – 1996) has a very special link with Rennes because it was where he lived in exile during the 1970s, before the fall of the dictatorship in 1974. The 'Carnation Revolution' meant the return to his country of the simple foreign language assistant, as he then was, at the University of Rennes 2. He came back several years later - as prime minister of Portugal! This also brings to mind the period spent at the same university by the Czech writer, Milan Kundera, who was also a fugitive from his own country. Just two famous figures among hundreds of anonymous others from all over the world - Africa, south-east Asia, eastern Europe, for instance – who bear witness to the tradition of welcome offered by Brittany and Rennes to political refugees of no matter what background.

Stendhal

"As I knew that Rennes had been completely destroyed by fire in 1720, I didn't expect to find anything interesting with regards to its architecture. **I was agreeably surprised.", wrote Stendhal** in *Mémoires d'un touriste*. The Opéra, the interior of the Parlement, the church of Sainte*(sic)*-Melaine, and the chapel of Saint-Yves grabbed his attention without taking the edge off his critical sharpness. "They were building a bridge over the Vilaine, which, there, is a really small river. I was very happy with my walks in the Thabor and the Mail. The conscripts were being taught how to handle their weapons, and their red trousers went beautifully with the setting sun. It was like a Canaletto painting."

Stivell

Alan Stivell, born Alain Cochevelou, is associated with the revival of Breton music in the 1970s, following in the wake of Glenmor. He is also behind the Renaissance of that magical instrument, the Celtic harp. Alongside current artists, such as Gilles Servat and the group Tri Yann, he has enlivened and helped to promote Breton music as a whole. And the movement has never faltered. Witness the popularity of Dan Ar Braz, Denez Prigent, Didier Squiban and so many others, who were often discovered at the *Tombées de la Nuit* festival in Rennes. The *Transmusicales*, another of Rennes' festivals, helped pave the way for the Rennes rock scene, which was led by Étienne Daho, Marquis de Sade, Marc Seberg, Niagara and, more recently, Billy ze Kick.

(Scene Rennaise) The Rennes Arts Scene

◁ **'La Cour des Grands' by J. Deschamps and M. Makeleff at the Théâtre National de Bretagne.**
D. Levasseur.

▷ **'Don Pasquale' by Donizetti at the Opera House.**
F. Galbrun.

▽ **'Penelope' by G. Fauré at the Opera House.**
D. Levasseur.

△ **'Madame Butterfly' by Puccini at the Opera House.**
F. Galbrun.

▷ **'The Marriage of Figaro' by Beaumarchais, directed by J.-F. Sivadier at the Théâtre National de Bretagne.**
TNB, A. Dugas.

▷ **A summer concert at the Triangle with th Orchestre de Bretagne conducted by S. Sanderling.**
R. Volante.

◁ **Jacques Higelin in concert at the Liberté.**
D. Levasseur.

◁◁ **'Les Voiles Ecarlates' (Scarlet Sails), a show by the Formann Brothers, at the Dromesko cabaret-theatre**
TNB, J. Ptacek.

(Scene Rennaise)
The Rennes Arts Scene

△ **The 'Campo, Vampo, Tacky' exhibition at the Criée contemporary art centre.** D. Levasseur.

▽ **The 'Fondations' (Foundations) exhibition at the Musée de Bretagne.** D. Levasseur.

△ **The Caravaggio exhibition at the Musée de Beaux-Arts.** D. Levasseur.

▽ **The Emmanuel Le Ray exhibition at the town planning information centre.** D. Levasseur.

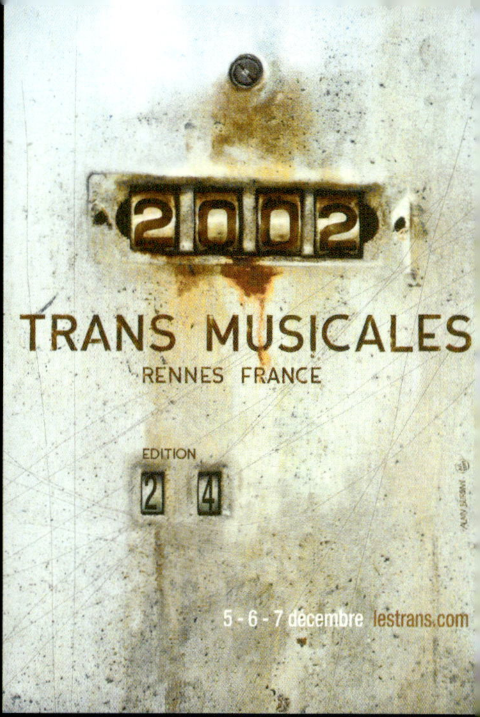

Alain Burban

atrapi

DR

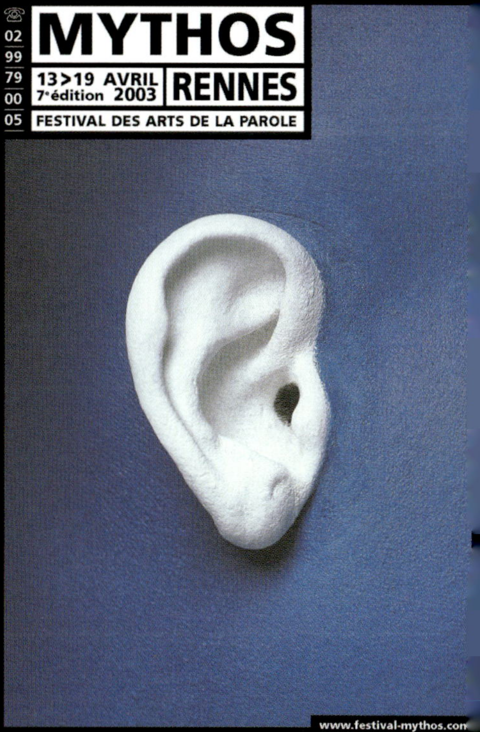

DR

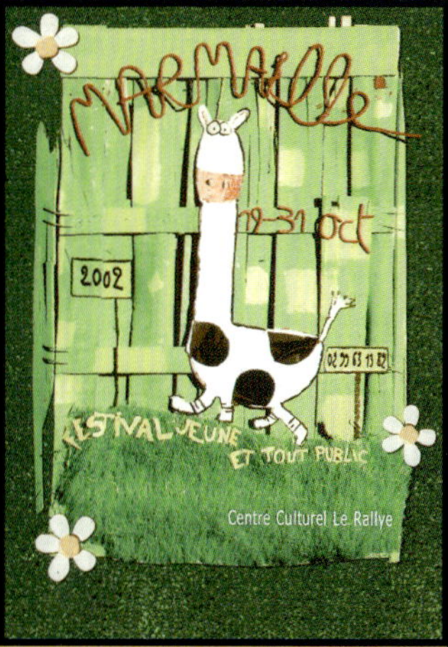

DR

T/U

Triangle

Surrounded by tower blocks, **it rose up from the ground in 1985,** on a piece of wasteland and in the form of ... a triangle, an ambitious project which was the fruit of 8 years of careful consideration and consultation with local residents. Today the Triangle cultural centre has been officially recognised by the Ministry of Culture for its work in the field of dance. It also provides a range of social and cultural activities and houses a library and the local branch of the 'mairie'. These facilities, perhaps less impressive but just as active, exist just about everywhere throughout the city, providing a mix of cultural and locally-based activities. This exceptional network of MJCs (Maisons des Jeunes et de la Culture – local community centres) means that Rennes certainly provides some of the best facilities of this kind of any city in France.

The Triangle also houses a local branch library.

The Multicultural Festival in May, 2001.

Ubu

The 'Ubu' concert venue, just across the road from the Lycée Emile Zola, where Alfred Jarry was a student.

"If that's the way it is, I'll push off. I'm going to kill everybody, and then push off." Before Ubu came Hébert, Félix Hébert, a physics teacher at today's Lycée Emile Zola when Alfred Jarry, the writer and creator of the character of Ubu in his books, *Ubu Roi, Ubu Enchaîné,* and *Ubu Cocu*, was a pupil there between 1888 and 1891. For the young lad from Laval and his friends, Hébert symbolised universal foolishness, and they immortalised him in a play which became, in 1896, the famous *Ubu Roi*.
Opposite the school on the Avenue Janvier, the Ubu modern music venue perpetuates the memory of this literary creation whose roots lie in the real life of Rennes.

Vanel (Charles) and Vattier (Robert)

The person who has long been regarded as **as the doyen of French cinema was from Rennes.** Charles Vanel was born in the Breton capital, studying at the Collège Saint-Martin before beginning a career, first of all in the theatre, and then in the cinema, with a leading role at the age of 20 years. He has an impressive filmography, with over 150 films, among which *Le Salaire de la Peur* directed by Henri-Georges Clouzot, which won him the title of best actor at the Cannes Festival in 1953, is especially memorable. Charles Vanel died in 1989.
Robert Vattier is better known by the name of 'Monsieur Brun', who became famous because of his appearance in Marcel Pagnol's trilogy, *César, Marius,* and *Fanny*. It is a little-known fact that this supposed native of Lyons was actually a Breton, being born in Rennes in 1906 and dying in Paris in 1982.
Other actors have links with Rennes, either because they were born there, e.g. Marcel Bozuffi (1929 – 1988) and Isabel Otero, or because, like Elisabeth Bourgine, they lived there.
Film directors from Rennes are somewhat fewer in number, comprising Jean-Luc Miesch, who made *Nestor Burma* and Christian Lejalé, and, unlike Nantes, few full-length films, apart from Christian Lejalé's *Loulou Graffiti* in 1991, have been made in the city.

Both the actors Robert Vattier ('Monsieur Brun' in Pagnol's films), and Charles Vanel (pictured here in « Les Diaboliques » were born in Rennes.
Collection Ronan Dantec

V

(Vélo) Bicycle

Behind the slogan of **"Rennes aime la petite reine"** (Rennes likes the little queen) lies the reality of the fact that the Breton capital has a certain fondness for the bicycle, with 150 km of 'green routes' (cycle paths and tracks as well as bus lanes) enabling cyclists to move around the city. In addition, a series of cycle parks with 200 cycles, which are available free of charge for use by the people of Rennes through a system of smart cards, has been set up by the firm of Dauphin Adshel. The bicycle also makes its presence felt in terms of sport, with the grand Prix Cycliste and many local cycle races, as well as with the Cyclades Rennaises festival.

(Verres et Céramiques) Glass and Ceramics

The Glass and Ceramics Research Centre, run by Jacques Lucas, has made Rennes one of the **the leading world centres for research into the chemistry of glass.** Since the 1970s, even before the existence as such of this centre, researchers explored solid fluoridated compounds and discovered new fluoride glass whose special properties were applied to telecommunications technology.

A decade later, Zhang, a young Chinese researcher, discovered TeX glass, a new material for use in infrared cameras, and it was he who, for instance, developed systems for measuring temperatures by remote control, analysing the process of fermentation in the agrochemical and food processing sectors, and detecting tumour formation on cells.

The centre has a staff of 50, and works with, among others, INSERM in medical research, Alcatel in telecommunications, and the Direction Générale de l'Armement (weapons) in infrared aiming systems. It has a highly developed network of links with, for example, Europe, the USA (Florida and Arizona universities), and Japan (Kyoto, Sapporo, and Sendai universities).

(Vierge) Virgin

The Bretons are particularly devoted in their worship of the Virgin Mary. The many statues of the Virgin, especially in Rennes city centre, provide a good illustration of this, as throughout the ages, the people of Rennes were in the habit of putting themselves under their protection. The creation of these niches for the Virgin was often linked to the great fire of 1720, but was also associated with cholera epidemics.

(Vivre en intelligence) Living intelligently

« Living intelligently / Living on good terms with each other ». Rennes' slogan in its communication campaigns since 1992, actually has a double meaning. Firstly, it pays tribute to all the concentration of brainpower in the universities, research laboratories, and businesses within the Rennes region. It is also, however, a recognition of the capacity of the people of Rennes to talk and work together, something that goes far beyond their differences of belief and opinion.

RENNES
VIVRE EN INTELLIGENCE

Vouziers

Vouziers is a town in the Ardennes region which suffered a great deal during the First World War, and which Rennes adopted in January 1919 in order to take a special interest in it. Strangely enough, Vouziers was also the birthplace of Jean Robic, the famous Breton racing cyclist (1921 - 1980), who won the Tour de France in 1947.

W

Waldeck-Rousseau (Pierre)

The creator of the 1901 law concerning non-profit-making organisations began his political career in Rennes as the deputy for Ille-et-Vilaine.

The father of the important 'Loi de 1901', concerning the setting up of non-profit-making organisations, fought his first political campaign here. Pierre Waldeck-Rousseau was born in Nantes in 1846, became a lawyer in Rennes in 1873, and very quickly headed the city's leading legal practice. The only Republican candidate, he was elected in 1879 to represent Ille-et-Vilaine in the National Assembly, the beginning of a brilliant political career which culminated in his becoming the Président du Conseil (Prime Minister) in 1899. It was during this period in office that his famous law was passed.

Today, he would certainly be delighted with the situation in Rennes, as the city is well-known for the vitality of its clubs and societies, of which there are an estimated 5,000. Since the 1950s and 1960s, the Breton capital has also had certain organisations, or 'offices', that are peculiar to it, such as the Office Social et Culturel (social and cultural life), the Office des Sports (sport), and the Office des Personnes à la Retraite (retired people), which act as umbrella organisations for the various clubs and societies, negotiate with the city council, and even manage the allocation of some of the grants. This grouping of organisations has been strengthened by the establishment of 'maisons' (centres), such as the Maison de la Consommation et de l'Environnement' (consumer advice and environmental matters), the Maison de la Santé (health), the Maison Internationale (international links, especially with Rennes' twin cities), and the Maison du Théâtre Amateur, as well as, more recently, by the appearance of 'collectives', such as the Jardin Moderne for contemporary music, and Skeudenn Bro Roazon for Breton culture.

Z.A.C.

Public control of the planning process has probably been the main characteristic of town planning in Rennes since the 1950s, during the mayoralties of both Henri Fréville (1953 – 1977) and Edmond Hervé (1977 -). This functions by, among other measures, total control of the land planning process, and, at the operational stage, by the frequent application of the provisions for Z.A.C.s **('zone d'aménagement concerté' – mixed housing development zone)** of which there are currently 27 in Rennes. This planning tool enables 25% of all city housing programmes to be made up of social housing units, whether they be situated in the city centre or on the outskirts.

Index

Translator

Valérie Sykes, A.I.L.

Photographic research

Réjane Guyomard
Claudine Piault

Photographs

City Archives (J.-C. Pigeon: pp. 9 (top), 27 (middle), 45 (top)
Departmental Archives (P. Bidel): pp. 19 (bottom), 20 (top), 27 (bottom), 45 (bottom)
Artefacto: p. 35 (top)
Rennes Public Library: pp. 4, 44 (middle)
Private collection: p. 8 (top left)
Fire Service Collection: pp. 19, 23 (top)
Erwann Pemptroad (Rennes City Council Map Department): map, pp. 40 - 41
Gilbert Lebrun: p. 47 (top)
Hedi El Boughammi: pp. 22, 58 (top) (middle)
Michel Ogier: pp. 7 (bottom), 18, (bottom), 58 (middle)
Musée de Bretagne (G. Prudor): pp. 13 (bottom left), 15 (bottom), 19 (middle), 23 (top), 36 (top), 37 (bottom), 42 (middle), 43 (bottom), 62 (top)
Musée de Beaux-Arts: pp. 35 (bottom), 39 (top)
Photo Bretagne Edition (R. Busch): pp. 8 (top right), 9 (bottom)
Rennes Métropole: p. 34
Richard Volante: pp. 6, 12 (Ecomusée de Rennes Collection), 13 (top), 14 (bottom), 15 (top), 20 (middle), 21 (top), 26, 29 (bottom), 37 (top), 38 (top), 43 (top), 46 (top and bottom), 50 (top)
Editions Rue des Scribes: p. 21
Rennes City Council Information Service (D. Levasseur): pp. 5, 14 (top), 18, 23 (bottom), 28, 29 (middle), 36 (bottom), 42 (top and bottom, 44, (top), 45 (middle), 46 (middle), 47 (bottom), 50 (bottom), 52 (bottom), 61

Published by Editions Ouest-France, Rennes
Layout: Editions Ouest-France graphic studio
Photoengraving: Scann'Ouest, Rennes
Printed by Pollina (printers) in Luçon (85) n° L48412
I.S.B.N. 978-2-7373-3046-9 - Publisher's number: 4402.03.03.10.08